COASTERS
in Focus

—— by ——
Bernard McCall

Bernard McCall

COASTERS in Focus

FOREWORD

On 18 May 1980, the author and I travelled together to Eastham on the River Mersey. This was my introduction to the hitherto unsuspected world of the shipping enthusiast.

He and I first became friends many years before when, as students, we shared a common enthusiasm for the steam locomotive. This enthusiasm led to many journeys across the length and breadth of Britain in order to photograph steam, many talks about "the old days" tinged with not a little nostalgia, and a bond between us which the passing years and distance have not severed. During that time, it was only gradually that I came to suspect that an even greater passion gripped him - ships.

Looking back at that drive to Eastham, where the Manchester Ship Canal meets the Mersey, my scepticism seems barely credible now. "Why ships?" I remember thinking to myself. "They don't 'live' in the way that a steam locomotive lives: no sound and fury; no steam and moving parts; no romance." Needless to say, these doubts about the trip lasted about as long as it took a chemical tanker called LOTOS to negotiate the locks and proceed to sea. The fascination of that sight has stayed with me ever since.

But to return to that question: "Why ships?" Maybe if you have casually picked up this book, the question has occurred to you as well. Think of the variety of ships which visit these islands: some large and some small; some graceful and some ugly; some old and some new. Think then of man's technological inventiveness in design pitted against the elemental forces of wind and tide. Think also of the human dimension: the camaraderie of those who work by or on the sea, born of shared adversity and mutual aid - tugmen and sea captains, pilots and boatmen, coastguards and dockers, radio controllers and agents. Think of ships with strange-sounding foreign names, from ports far away, and of the romance of long journeys just beginning and of safe returns to home waters. Think of a community in which you, as an enthusiast, might become involved.

In the pages that follow, each reader will find his or her own responses but what all cannot fail to notice is the enthusiasm of the author. He and his camera, indeed his whole family, are indefatigable in recording the maritime scene. He is fond of saying that apparently humdrum views today can, with the passage of a few years, become historic. Ships are lost or go to the breakers, ports close, trading patterns change - capturing all these things is part of his quest.

In this quest, I have seen yachts, chimneys, cranes, long grass, clouds that obscure the sun, jetties, seagulls and even traffic lights incur his wrath if they, singly or collectively, attempt to spoil a view of a shipping subject. He has charmed the most recalcitrant security guards, extracted permits from unwilling port authorities, arranged trips on pilot boats, received offers of coastal voyages and created a network of information sources in the shipping world which is most impressive. He has been known to travel 500 miles and more for one ship movement and, perhaps his greatest achievement, has converted past unbelievers like me. It is therefore a considerable honour that some of my photographs should appear in these pages. It is also a tribute to the unselfishness with which he shares his enthusiasm and his knowledge.

Why ships? Read on - the bug may bite you too!

Ian Willett
Epping, April 1990

BRITISH SHIPOWNERS

One of the saddest features of the shipping scene in recent years has been the decline of the British merchant fleet. In this opening section, we look at a few of the survivors in the coastal trades, and we begin with two companies whose headquarters are on the east coast. The Trent-based J. Wharton (Shipping) Ltd. celebrates its centenary in 1990, and our first view shows the suitably-named TRENTONIA heading up the Humber and bound for her "home" river. Built at Goole in 1964, she served Wharton for 20 years before being sold to other British owners and renamed TRENTON (see p. 54). The photograph was taken on 7 March 1982.

Her sistership ECCTONIA was built at the same yard but in 1963 and she is seen in pristine condition on 21 February 1982 at Goole, her home port. She is one of my favourite vessels, and since 1987 has traded as VASA SOUND for Kirkwall-based Dennison Shipping, a firm which has gone against the trend and expanded its fleet.

Based in Hull is J. Rix and Sons Ltd., a firm which has often enjoyed success in placing its coasters in long-term contracts rather than face the vicissitudes of the spot charter market. On the south coast of the U.K., Rix ships have been active in the stone and china clay trades. Arriving at Par on 7 August 1981 to load the latter commodity is FYLRIX She was built at Appingedam in 1962. On 21 November 1984, while bound from Dean Quarry to London with stone, she suffered a severe list when off the Eddystone Lighthouse and subsequently sank in Jennycliff Bay.

JEMRIX was built for a different Hull company, Hull Gates, in 1965 as IRISHGATE. She was thus named for she operated a container service to Ireland from Garston. Sold to Rix in 1974, she then spent several years transporting steel from Ijmuiden to U.K. ports such as Whitby, Rochester and King's Lynn. She is seen here leaving Cardiff bound for Spain with a cargo of scrap. Just visible on top of her wheelhouse is a compass adjuster at work. Since the photograph was taken on 30 January 1988, her flag has been changed to that of the Bahamas as a cost-cutting measure.

Some British companies have merged in order to survive. An example is that of tne Liverpool-based S. William Coe and Thomas J. Metcalf. Vessels from each fleet have maintained their traditional colours and nomenclature. We begin with two ships from the Coe fleet whose vessels continue to be active in the coal trade to Ireland and in stone traffic. In the Mersey on 1 June 1971 is MAYTHORN, built in Holland in 1962. She was renamed BRINDLE in 1981, and WILGO a year later. She changed her British flag for that of Malta in 1985 when she became MONARCH PRIDE, and was scrapped in Spain later that year.

FIRETHORN, also built in Holland but in 1967, is currently in the fleet and is seen here arriving at Swansea to load coal on 20 April 1979.

The Metcalf firm dates back to 1924 when Thomas J. Metcalf purchased his first vessel. The firm's cargo ships were, like Coe's, regularly involved in the coal trade. Seen in the Mersey on 14 June 1980, the Burntisland-built EILEEN M dates from 1966. She left the fleet in 1984 following her sale to Cayman Island-flag operators who renamed her CAERLEON although the original intention had been to call her CELT PIONEER. A report in 1986 that she had reverted to her original name seems erroneous. She was laid-up awaiting repairs at Mamonal in April 1986 and was still there over a year later, since when her fate is something of a mystery.

The Metcalf contributions to the current fleet are all tankers, and the vessel with the most unusual profile, in that her bridge is amidships, is ROBERT M. Built as CREE in Hong Kong in 1970 for use in Far Eastern waters, she joined the Metcalf fleet in 1977. She can carry bitumen, and until recently, has been mostly used conveying that substance between Stanlow and Ardrossan. The photograph was taken as she approached Eastham on 3 September 1977.

Vessels in the fleet of Comben Longstaff bore names ending with the suffix BROOK. CAERNARVONBROOK, seen at Eastham on 30 September 1973, was built at Wallsend in 1964. She was sold in 1976, to be renamed MERIDIAN SKY. She took the names CYCLADES and then STAR in 1979. Laid-up at Piraeus in November 1981, she was still there 18 months later. She was reported to have been renamed EFTYCHIA in 1984 but she is another vessel whose subsequent career details are yet to emerge.

LANCASTERBROOK dates from 1975 and was built in Holland. She was photographed in Rotterdam's Botlek area on 26 May 1980. She had a spell under the name CHELSEASTREAM between 1977 and 1979, and, to illustrate the fact that ship ownership is a complex business in every sense of that word, she has had various nominal owners including Midland Montagu Leasing Ltd. In the early 1980s, the Comben Longstaff title disappeared as the management of LANCASTERBROOK and her three sisterships moved to F. T. Everard whose funnel colours were applied to the ships in place of the traditional "C L."

F. T. EVERARD AND SONS LTD.

One of the largest fleet of coasters under the British flag has always been that operated by this Thames-based family company. Both tankers and dry cargo ships have made up the fleet, and the next four pages depict a selection of vessels operated during the last two decades. We begin with a couple of tankers. One of the more recent additions to the fleet is AMITY which is seen about to leave Barry on 24 September 1989. Built in Japan in 1980, she traded as CHRISTIAN until 1988.

Another South Wales view with the Goole-built AUDACITY, dating from 1968, approaching Cardiff on 23 May 1986.

On this page, we look at two vessels no longer in the fleet. CAPACITY was built by J. Pollock at Faversham in 1963, and was photographed four years later in the New Waterway near Rotterdam.

It was double stamps at Goole on 17 July 1978. In the background is WILLIAM J. EVERARD, built in 1963, and in the foreground is GEORGINA V. EVERARD, dating from 1955; both ships were built at Goole. The former was sold in 1982 and converted to a drilling ship named WIMPEY GEOCORE. Four years earlier, GEORGINA V. was sold to Lebanese owners and renamed MYASSAR. I am uncertain about her subsequent fate - she may still be trading in the Lebanon and Middle East. But I have no ambition to go there to find out!

Two other female members of the family are found on this page. In the upper picture, MAIRI EVERARD is seen from the Humber Bridge on 27 April 1984 when she was bound for the River Trent with a cargo of timber. Shortly before this book went to press, it was reported that she had been sold to the Cowes-based Carisbrooke Shipping Ltd. and renamed GRETA C. She was built at Wallsend in 1974. It was ten years later that PAMELA EVERARD (below) was built at Lowestoft. She was photographed off Portishead on 14 February 1988.

otographed from the Humber Bridge as she passed her birthplace at Hessle on 27 April 1984 is the
71-built SINCERITY. She hoisted the Cypriot flag as WILLEM W in 1986.

We close this section of British shipowners as we began it, with mention of J. Wharton (Shipping) Ltd.
COMITY was built at Selby in 1980 as ANGELONIA for the Wharton firm, moving to the Everard fleet in
1988. The photograph was taken on 5 August 1988 as she was passing the Hook of Holland, bound for
Rotterdam. Beyond the breakwater is the Caland Canal and beyond that can be discerned a large tanker
at Europoort.

CHINA CLAY

This commodity accounts for a great percentage of the export cargo from ports in Devon and Cornwall, with most of the clay being shipped through the three ports in St. Austell Bay which are featured in this section. We begin with the most westerly and smallest of the three - Charlestown. With loading completed, BREYDON TRADER makes ready to leave on 30 March 1989. Built at Emden in 1967 as ANTON HELD, she took her present name in 1986.

The three loading chutes are visible in this view of SUSAN W on 19 April 1985. This immaculately-kept vessel dated from 1958 when she was built at Stade as KATHE AHRENS, becoming GESINE P in 1970, both under the West German flag. In late 1984, she hoisted the British flag, but it was to prove only a brief life thus for she was gutted by fire off the Hook of Holland on 8 October 1985 when bound for Europoort from Selby. Readers may wish to scrutinise this view and speculate where I was standing to photograph BREYDON TRADER!

The port of Par is best visited in the late afternoon when not only have ships completed a day's loading, but also the sun is in just the right position to illuminate vessels entering and leaving the port. The rust-streaked DON RICARDO approaches the entrance on 14 April 1987. This ship has kept her original name since her construction by J. J. Sietas in 1967.

Photographed on the same tide and from the same vantage point but looking towards the tidal dock, EGRET has the assistance of the pilot cutter as she prepares to swing. The clay dries are prominent in the background. This ship is interesting in that she was built in West Berlin. Launched as A. HELD in 1966, she was lengthened in 1973. She was renamed MOON TRADER in 1979 and then CORMORANT and EGRET in 1986 - one wonders about the uncertainty as to which bird to use.

At the beginning of a fully-laden voyage from Par to Antwerp on 30 July 1981 is BOBRIX. She was built at Groningen in 1957, and met her end when on passage from Bordeaux to Teignmouth on 14 November 1981. Her hatch covers became dislodged during a heavy storm, resulting in her sinking but fortunately without loss of life.

The setting of the port of Fowey is spectacular. Its deep water enables ships of up to 10,000 tonnes capacity to use its facilities. Cargoes are exported world-wide, but in particular to Scandinavia and the Mediterranean. The latter is the eventual destination of the Spanish ARAMIL, photographed loading on 2 August 1981. Of classic bridge-amidships profile, she was built at Gijon in 1963. Scrapped in Greece in 1986, she is the third of the vessels in this section to have kept her original name throughout her life.

With the loading facilities in almost constant use, it is common to find ships anchored in the harbour awaiting their turn. On 27 March 1989, the Polish ZGORZELEC was one of no less than 14 ships in port and was photographed from one of the popular self-drive hire boats. This ship was built by Ferguson Bros., Port Glasgow, in 1980.

The slipway leading to the small ferry at Bodinnick is just visible by the stern of the Swedish SARAH as she departs on 30 March 1989. Another Sietas-built ship, she dates from 1971.

RIVERS GREAT . . .

Rivers may be considered "great" by virtue of their fame, rather than length, depth or volume of trade. This short selection is personal, and I begin with the Thames. Passing Tilbury Landing Stage on 18 February 1980 is WOOLACOMBE, a British coaster whose origins are clearly Dutch. She was built as CLARISSA at Martenshoek in 1967, her name change coming in 1977. Tilbury and Gravesend are popular places for ship viewing.

The Tyne is illustrated by a familiar caller of yesteryear. STORMONT, seen heading for Newcastle Quay on 5 August 1975, was built as FIFE COAST for Coast Line in 1954 at George Brown's Greenock yard. She was renamed FRUIN in 1958 and STORMONT in 1963. In 1976 she was sold to Lebanese owners, renamed RABUNION VII, and was subsequently converted to a livestock carrier. In this guise she continues to trade in the Mediterranean and Middle East.

Much of my early ship spotting was done on the Mersey, and the atmosphere of that river and its environs is unique. My illustration is dated 1 November 1973 and shows the Irish vessel CORK whose career began in 1937 when she was constructed by the Dublin Dockyard Co. as KILKENNY, her name change occurring in 1971. On 25 May 1974, she suffered a severe engine breakdown when off Holyhead. Repairs being uneconomical, she was sold to shipbreakers at Dalmuir.

As far as commercial trade is concerned, one of the world's most important waterways is that formed by the arteries of the rivers Rhine, Maas and Lek, and which is termed the New Waterway. It is most appropriate, therefore, that we find, on 31 May 1985, SEA MAAS passing the 0 kilometre post as she heads along the New Waterway towards the sea. Built in Poland in 1974, she joined the Glenlight fleet in 1986 and, now fitted with a movable deck crane, she trades as GLENCLOY and is a familiar sight in the ports of the western U.K.

. . . AND SMALL

Once again, a personal selection. We begin on the River Nene, with the 1955-built TERENCE at Wisbech on 29 May 1982. She took this name in 1982, having had 5 previous identities since her construction by J. J. Sietas. In turn, she was KLAUS BLOCK, SUDERELV, TILLA DORIS, DOLORIS and LETICIA.

The 1980s saw a significant increase in the number of ships sailing to the various wharves on the River Usk. Although sand dredgers discharge still further upriver, Blaina Wharf is the most inland wharf used by conventional coasters. The Bristol Channel is noted for its extreme tidal range, a fact illustrated by the view of ELISABETH HOLWERDA at Blaina Wharf on 15 February 1984. The ship dates from 1975 and was built at Stroobos in Holland. In 1987, she became ELINA B under the Cypriot flag.

Although I was born and brought up only a few miles from the port of Preston, it is to my lasting regret that I took so few photographs there. Approaching the docks from the River Ribble on 12 February 1978 is the Cypriot ARCO. Constructed in Spain in 1966, she had already had the names LA RABIDA and LA CINTA. In 1984, she became ASSOS ENA, in 1986, POLYGON and AGATHA M. As such, she flew the Sri Lankan flag but traded in the Mediterranean. She hoisted the Maltese flag as AVGI in 1989.

Since reopening in 1979, the port of Fosdyke on the River Welland has seen trade increase considerably. Photographed there on 2 August 1989 was the St. Vincent-flagged VIBEKE. She had had no less than 7 previous names since her construction in Denmark in 1966. This was to be her last, though, for she was abandoned by her crew and sank on 26 November 1989 during heavy weather when on passage from Leixoes to Colchester.

RIVER ELBE

A minicruise to Hamburg is highly recommended for anyone with an interest in ships. One passes a wide variety of shipping during the voyage along the Elbe.

Our first view is near the mouth of the river and shows the West German DANIA-CARINA on 30 May 1984. Built by J. J. Sietas at Hamburg as APOLLO in 1957, she was renamed in 1977. In 1984, she became CHRISTA KERSTIN and, by coincidence, she was a regular caller at the port of Fosdyke under the command of her owner, Captain Jaeger.

Of much more modern design is JAN-V of 1985 and built at Duisburg. She was photographed when hurrying towards Hamburg on 29 May 1986.

On the previous page, there was little evidence of industrial or residential background. On the southern bank, near the estuary, is the town of Cuxhaven. Passing the harbour entrance on 27 May 1979 is the Danish tanker BELLAN FIRE. She was built at Rendsburg as TERKOL in 1963. Between 1965 and 1977, she traded for Esso as ESSO RONNE. She was then renamed BELLAN IV, this being restyled to BELLAN FIRE in 1979. Within a year, she left northern European waters for the Mediterranean after being sold to Greek owners and renamed MARK XIV, thus having a "numerical" name for the second time in her career. She was sold within Greece in 1985 and renamed MARIO.

It was at Flensburg that JADE was built in 1965. She was launched as MIGNON, and was named FRANZ HELD between 1970 and 1982. The photograph was taken on 29 May 1986. Ship enthusiasts will doubtless cast envious glances at the properties on the river bank!

WHERE DID YOU SAY?

In the introduction to my ''Coasters around Britain,'' I described my project, begun in 1972, to photograph a ship at every port in Britain. That book contained a selection of photographs of coasters in the small ports. The project is not yet completed, but a further 4 ports are featured here.

The tiny jetty at Barcaldine on Loch Creran, north-east of Oban, sees only very occasional traffic. The usual caller is Gardner's SAINT ORAN with a liquid chemical cargo for the Kelco plant. However, once or twice per year a consignment of dried seaweed is brought, a cargo which Dennison Shipping's CALF SOUND has transported from her home port of Kirkwall. She was built in 1969 by J. R. Hepworth at Paull as BLATENCE for Crescent Shipping. A simple name change saw her trading as LATEN in 1985, and she joined the Dennison fleet the next year. She met a premature end on 25 September 1989 when she sank during a voyage from Berwick-upon-Tweed to Kirkwall after her cargo of cement had shifted.

Fingringhoe is on the River Colne, a few miles downstream from Colchester. No longer do small coasters navigate the tiny creek to the flour mill here, but Ballast Quay on the south bank of the river is still used for exports of sand. Much of this is taken to the Thames by small vessels owned by J. J. Prior Ltd. In the foreground of this view is the 1961-built BERT PRIOR. Of more interest, though, is PETER P. She was built at Sunderland in 1915 as an Admiralty X lighter named X57, one of a series of craft used in the Gallipoli landings. Obviously much-altered since those days, it is nevertheless a pleasure to find a vessel with such an interesting history still trading.

Hoo Creek lies just off the River Medway. The small town's wharf does not handle cargo but, in addition to being the headquarters of the thriving coaster operator R. Lapthorn & Co., it is used by small vessels for lay-up and repair purposes. On 12 August 1989, we see LOBE in the foreground, now being repaired and refurbished by Medway-based owners Alan and Annette Pratt, and ROINA is just visible in the background.

On the south bank of the Humber, Killingholme has had a tanker jetty for many years. In the late 1980s, a wharf was opened for cargo handling and, like other wharves in this area, it dries out at low water. Discharging coal on 2 August 1989 is the West German HERMOD, a name she took earlier in the year after being named HERM J since her construction at Emden in 1980.

THESE ARE A FEW OF MY FAVOURITE PORTS.

What makes a ''favourite'' port? It may be the geographical setting, the type of ships, or the warmth of the welcome. In the case of the Kent port of Whitstable, it is the latter. Trade is dominated by the import of aggregates, a cargo which can be seen in the hold of EAU DE VIE on 7 August 1988. Built at Wallsend in 1968, she traded as FORMALITY for F. T. Everard until 1987 when she was purchased by Alan and Annette Pratt. They sold her in mid-1988 and she was renamed THAMESWOOD. A swirling sea mist off the harbour entrance has hidden the horizon in this view.

There is always much of shipping interest in the inlets and creeks of the Medway. Rochester itself, with its wharves and shipyards, is a popular haunt for coaster enthusiasts. With the railway bridge in the middle distance hiding the A2 road bridge, we look at 4 ships, including the contrasting sterns of 3 former Crescent Shipping vessels. Sandwiched between LIBATION and ROFFEN, which we shall see again on pages 66/67, is LOACH, built by Bay Wharf Construction Co., London, in 1968. To the far right is MEDWAY TRADER, a vessel we shall catch up with on p. 34. The photograph was taken on 12 August 1989.

Glasson Dock, at the mouth of the River Lune, has experienced fluctuating fortunes since its opening in 1783. However, current trade is thriving with much cargo heading for the Isle of Man. The Ramsey Steamship Company's BEN AIN is leaving the port for the island on 25 July 1989. Built in Holland as DEBEN for Blue Star Line in 1966, she became GRETCHEN WESTON in 1971 and took her present name in 1976.

The busy Devon port of Teignmouth looks set to prosper still further following the closure of the nearby port of Exmouth. Leaving Teignmouth on 31 March 1989 is the attractive ALCION, whose history will be outlined when we see her again on page 45.

. . . AND SHIPS

We stay at Teignmouth, looking from Shaldon, but we pan to the right and find SALOME outward bound to Shoreham on 18 April 1982. Registered in Colon, Panama, she will be recognisable to some readers as a former Everard ship. Built in 1955 at Wallsend, she traded as CONTINUITY for 22 years. She still survives, though she has been laid up at Iddefjord since June 1986.

We move to another holiday resort, Scarborough, for a view of MAY MITCHELL arriving with a cargo of potatoes on 23 August 1979. Of classic Dutch design with "acorn-topped" masts, she was built at Delfzijl in 1950 as REMA. Her other names were LERWICK and CORBIERE before she joined the Thames-based Mitchell fleet in 1971. Ten years later, she was sold to Panamanian-flag operators and was eventually demolished in February 1985.

Also built in Delfzijl but in 1957 was MARTENSHOEK, which became BEREND N in 1970, HOOPRIDE in 1974 and HOOP in 1984. As such we see her entering the Gloucester Ship Canal at Sharpness during a downpour on 17 May 1987. She became HELEN in 1989.

Yet another classic Dutch coaster is MARY COAST, built at Appingedam in 1961 as VECHTBORG. She bore the names ESPERANCE, NOORDSTER and FINLANDIA prior to taking the name MARY COAST in 1985 when bought by skipper Derick Goubert. She traded regularly to the Channel Islands and it was to Jersey that she was bound with coal when photographed at Cardiff on 13 October 1988. In early 1990, she was sold to West Indies owners and renamed COMPASION DE L'ETERNAL.

FLATTIES OLD AND NEW

For many years, colliers were built with low superstructures and collapsible funnels so that they could navigate the Thames to up-river wharves. There are considerable economies to be had in delivering a cargo as closely as possible to its ultimate destination or collecting it from its source with a minimum amount of trans-shipment. In the 1970s, coasters began to appear with a substantial cargo capacity and boasting wheelhouses which could be raised and lowered hydraulically, and with collapsible masts. Having what is technically known as a low air draught, these ships are able to sail far inland on rivers and canals, even to places such as Basle, Liège, Lyon, Paris and Vienna. Our near-continental neighbours have learnt to use these vessels to excellent advantage. Sadly, the U.K. seems unable to formulate any transport policy whatsoever, let alone one which maximises the use of our navigable waterways.

CROYDON, seen (above) loading at Seaham in the mid-1960s, was built at Burntisland in 1951 for the South Eastern Gas Board. She left their ownership after 20 years valiant service, and then had a series of Mediterranean-based owners for whom she traded as ACYRO, CHRIS, MARO and VASILIS IV. To the best of my knowledge, she still survives.

Also built on the Firth of Forth but at Grangemouth in 1950 was KEYNES. She began life as ACCUM, working for the North Thames Gas Board, and was sold to Stephenson Clarke who renamed her KEYNES in 1967. She is seen at Newcastle Quay on 5 August 1975. Bought by Greek owners, she was renamed TITIKA and was eventually scrapped at Piraeus in February 1984.

One could almost turn this into a "Spot the Difference" puzzle page! Both vessels are leaving Shoreham in the summer of 1979.On 17 August, CLIMPING is committed to film as she departs in ballast.
She was built in 1958 as CAMBERWELL for the South Eastern Gas Board. Her builders were Hall Russell, Aberdeen, and she was Yard Number 864. She joined the Stephenson Clarke fleet in 1970 and served as CLIMPING for ten years before being eventually demolished in Spain.

Hall Russell's Yard Number 861 was built in 1957, also for the S.E.G.B., and was named DULWICH. She, too, joined Stephenson Clarke in 1970 and was renamed WORTHING. Unlike her sistership above, she found further buyers for she was sold to Cypriot owners in 1977 and, with a few dashes of the paintbrush, renamed WORTHY. We see her as such shortly before a further sale which resulted in her name being changed to ANTIGONE P. She arrived in Spain for demolition on Christmas Day, 1981. Readers may care to observe the photographs closely to see what modifications her Mediterranean owners made.

We now look at the new breed of "flatties". The two photographs on this page were taken from the Humber Bridge on 7 August 1983. (Above) we see the West German MARKAB, built at Haren/Ems in 1977. She hoisted the French flag in 1985 and is now renamed ARAMON.

Although the majority of the modern sea/river coasters have been built in West Germany, a substantial number have also been built in the Netherlands. This example has a fixed wheelhouse. She was built at Bergum in 1978 as THALASSA, and was renamed FRISIANA the next year. A decade later saw her name shortened to FRISIAN. Her crew and their family seem to be guarding the car from the attention of the photographer, although two others slumber on deck!

A stern view of the West German BALTICA taken from the Forth Bridge. She was built at Wewelsfleth in 1983 and must, therefore, have been new when photographed on 12 April of that year.

The forward-looking Crescent Shipping entered this sphere of coaster design with the construction of URGENCE and VIBRENCE at Selby in 1981. The latter leaves Par on 15 April 1985.

MANCHESTER SHIP CANAL

The terminal docks in Salford are being redeveloped, and very little maritime traffic now penetrates the upper reaches of the Canal although the lower section still remains busy. Passing the outskirts of the town of Ellesmere Port, the Dutch QUO VADIS hurries inland on 10 September 1972. This 1956-built ship was renamed MANOR PARK in 1978 and has been laid-up in the Medway at Chatham since 1 October 1988.

Leaving Irlam Locks on 4 June 1973 is Stephenson Clarke's tanker FERNHURST. Built at Blyth in 1961, she was sold and renamed DAVAK in 1983. Laid-up at Lisbon in 1984, she was subsequently demolished there.

The Ship Canal had a flourishing railway system to complement its work, and the tracks are visible in the foreground of this photograph of the Norwegian gas tanker LOTOS approaching Latchford Locks on the outskirts of Warrington in 1967. Dating from 1965 when she was built at Oslo, she became ONESTAR in 1974. In March 1984, she was laid-up at New Orleans. By mid-1988, it was reported that she was to be renamed WITSUPPLY and fly the British flag, but there seems to be no evidence of this change having taken place.

A different type of tanker, the British ESSO PURFLEET, is about to pass beneath Latchford High Level Bridge on 24 February 1979. She has had an eventful history since leaving the Esso fleet to be renamed PRIMA JEMINA in 1983. 1986 found her the subject of a judicial sale at Gibraltar when she was renamed THITA PEGASUS. In the next year, she was renamed RAINBOW and almost immediately DUBAI STAR under which name she continues to trade in the Middle East.

In the mid-1970s, a group of 5 vessels was built for Bulk Cargo Handling Services, a subsidiary of Alexandra Towing, for the carriage of cereals along the Canal. These cereals were transshipped from large bulk carriers at Liverpool. MERSEY TRADER was built at Bromborough in 1977, and is seen near Warrington on 24 February 1979. In the 1980s, the trading pattern changed, and the cereals were brought to Manchester by coaster usually from France (see p. 36). As a result, MERSEY TRADER and her 4 sisters were laid-up pending sale. In her case, it was late 1988 when she moved to Rochester and was laid-up as MEDWAY TRADER (see p. 24). Following a solitary voyage to Colchester, she arrived in London on 20 November and was again laid up.

From Runcorn Salt Works are exported the products of the vast Cheshire salt plain. Loading on 26 August 1979 was the West German HEIDE-CATRIN. In view of the frequency of name changes, it seems worth noting that she has kept her name since her construction in 1975 at the Hamburg yard of J. J. Sietas.

It is the stretch of the Canal from the entrance locks at Eastham, past Ellesmere Port and the oil installations at Stanlow, to Runcorn which now sees most activity. Approaching Stanlow in ballast on 26 August 1979 is Metcalf's FRANK M. She has surpassed HEIDE-CATRIN in that she has kept her name since she was built at Burntisland in 1965.

For our final Ship Canal view, we return to the upper reaches to find GILLIAN EVERARD at Trafford Wharf's grain silo on 10 September 1972. A 1963 product of Cleland's Wallsend shipyard, she was sold to Maltese interests in 1984, becoming CAPTAIN CHRISTOS G., and three years later she hoisted the Honduran flag as GEORGIOS. Although the ship survives, the industrial archaeology behind her has been flattened.

CEREALS

The transport of cereals by ship is an important feature of our trade. By and large, the trade consists of imports but there is a significant export market, too. Underway on the Manchester Ship Canal after leaving Irlam Locks on 6 November 1988 is INISHEER. She is bound for Cerestar Wharf at Trafford Park and is typical of the coasters which took over this trade from MERSEY TRADER and her sisters. Built in 1985 as ELISA VON BARSSEL, she had already borne the names FLAGSHIP 1 and LIA VENTURE.

Colour photographs would reveal that the two ships on this page have hulls of an identical light green hue. They are owned by different companies which come within the overall control of Arklow Shipping Ltd. SHEVRELL, built at Delfzijl in 1981, is discharging at Rank's Solent Mill in Southampton on 28 August 1983.

The River Tyne has mills owned by two of the major flour millers. On the north bank, we find (above) Union Transport's UNION JUPITER at the Spillers Mill on 27 April 1980. She was built in 1977 and was renamed PRION on 30 June 1989.

Joseph Rank's Gateshead Mill is on the south bank and WILHELMINA V was photographed here on 5 June 1982. She is operated by International Shipbrokers whose vessels are always kept in immaculate condition.

THAMWELL was photographed at the silos in Goole's South Dock on 21 February 1982.
Constructed at Martenshoek in 1963, she traded as VICTRESS for the well-known Groningen-based
coaster owners, Beck's, until 1981. In 1988, she was sold and renamed MAENPORTH, and two years later,
she was sold again, this time being renamed MARYSTAN.

Stambridge Mill at Rochford is at the limit of navigation on the River Roach in Essex. It towers above the
small coasters which call. A regular visitor in the late 1980s was ANGLIAN TRADER, dating from
1966, which spent the first ten years of her life as LADY SHEENA working for Thomas Watson of
Rochester. She bore the names SHEENA K, TARGET VENTURE and LEE JAMES before taking on her
current name in 1982. As this book goes to press, she is reported to have been renamed RAIDER. It is
worth noting that all six ships featured in this section were built in the Netherlands.

COLOURFUL COASTERS

In searching for a unifying theme for a colour section, it was not too difficult to come up with the idea of the different hull colours sported by coasters. Proving that black can be as attractive as any other colour, the Dutch ANNA MARIA hurries up the Elbe on 1 June 1989.
She was built as GISELA BARTELS in 1966 by H. Rancke at Hamburg, replacing an identically-named ship built four years earlier, and she was incidentally the last ship to be built at this yard. She became ESTE in 1975 and took her present name in 1980.

White is the usual colour for refrigerated ships, always known as reefers. Discharging potatoes at Barry on 5 June 1990 is POLAR, built in Finland in 1968 and renamed from POLAR SCAN in 1974.

Berwick-upon-Tweed is the setting for our next two ships. On 20 May 1989, CALF SOUND prepares
to load a cargo of palletised cement for her home port of Kirkwall. The cement originates from nearby
Dunbar and its export through Berwick is a recent revival since 1988.

Both photographs
by Ian Willett

At the same berth and loading an identical cargo on 30 September 1989 is the Danish OPNOR. Built
at Husum in 1962, she was originally named GERDA VESTA, and was renamed in 1964.

In the lower reaches of the Elbe, the Danish ANNE METTE is illuminated by the early morning sun on 3 June 1982. Built at Svendorg in 1972, she was sold to Italian owners in 1984 and renamed SILVANA.

It is usual to find tankers, whose liquid cargo is often hazardous, painted red or orange in order to maximise visibility. Yellow is less common, but it is noted on the liquid chlorine tanker NORTHERN STAR, which is usually to be found sailing between the Manchester Ship Canal and Maydown, near Londonderry. She was built in Norway in 1980, and we see her approaching Eastham on 12 August 1983.

HENRIK THOLSTRUP typifies the vivid hue of tankers. This liquefied gas tanker, built in the Netherlands in 1984, was originally named VINLAND under the Faroese flag and she was sold and renamed in 1987. She was photographed at Milford Haven on 12 February 1989.

Grey, albeit rust-streaked, is illustrated by Coe Metcalf's QUICKTHORN approaching Newlyn on 25 February 1989. The vessel dates from 1967 when she was built at the Troon yard of Ailsa Shipbuilders as TANMERACK. She joined the Coe fleet in 1973. In early 1990, she was sold to Maltese-flag owners and renamed AMANECIDA.

SAME OR DIFFERENT?

Ship identification can be made tricky by the fact that different vessels may have the same name and care has to be taken to ensure that a vessel is correctly identified. I have fallen victim to errors on more than one occasion! On this page we find two ships named ORION III. Above is the 1966 version, built at Husum and renamed LORE 1 in 1984. The photograph shows her in the Humber on 6 February 1982. Her more modern namesake was built at Emden in 1975 as HANSA and took the name ORION III in . . . 1984!. She was photographed, below, at Wisbech on 4 August 1988.

Each of these photographs was taken from the lock head at Goole. Being towed from the Dutch River into the Ouse on 13 February 1977 was the Danish SIVAL (above). Dating from 1958 when she was built at Busum, she stranded on 6 September 1977 when 25 km. south of Gothenburg and later sank, fortunately without loss of life. Her owner replaced her with a ship built at Husum in 1961 which had traded as REINHARD DANZ until 1969 and STEVNSBOEN until 1977. The photograph (below) was taken on 17 July 1978.

contrast, we often find the same ship but under different names. One of the reasons for providing in
is book the other names of each vessel is to offer the reader the opportunity of recalling a ship under a
evious name. ESPERO (top) dates from 1966 when she was built at Hoogezand and she had already had
o previous names, LUMEY and ESPERANCE, by the time this photograph was taken on 18 February
78 as she was outward bound in the River Trent. In 1979, she became VIOS and is again seen in the
ent (below) but inward bound in late 1980. With lowered masts, she is clearly prepared to pass beneath
e bridge at Gunness on her way to Gainsborough. In 1984, she was renamed NESCIO and, four years
ter became ALCION. We saw her so named on page 25.

46

Built in 1959 by the Ardrossan Dockyard Ltd., this coaster spent the first twenty years of her life working for Coast Lines as DORSET COAST. In 1979, she hoisted the Egyptian flag as EL HUSSEIN, under which identity she spent some time laid-up at Birkenhead. It was here that the photograph (top) was taken on 13 May 1979. In 1981, she was renamed EL KHEER and, shortly afterwards, DENTON VENTURE. As such, she is seen (bottom) in the River Ouse, outward bound from Goole on 15 April 1982. By 1984, she was renamed OURANIA, under which name I saw her at Piraeus that year, and she was scrapped at Bruges in mid-1985.

One for the classical scholars! The ships are clearly different - and so are the names. But the classicist will know that the goddess Pallas and the goddess Athene are one and the same. The upper photograph shows the Finnish PALLAS in the River Mersey in 1967. This fine vessel was built in 1953 at Alblasserdam. She went to Mediterranean owners in 1968 and was renamed ANITA, and then ANNA III some five years later. On 8 June 1975, she was laid up at Piraeus and, whilst there, was renamed ANNOULA K in 1977. She remained laid-up in 1979 and I assume was demolished some time during the next two years.

AROS ATHENE is an example of a highly successful design from J. J. Sietas. When launched in 1976, her name was ELBSTROM. She alternated between this name and AROS ATHENE no less than seven times during the next eleven years. The photograph was taken on 6 February 1982 when presumably the painter was taking a well-earned rest!. She broke the name pattern in 1987 by being renamed ERIKA, then she became ALYBELLE in 1988. She trades as such in mid-1990 - but for how long?! These two vessels lead us naturally to look at some more . . .

GODDESSES . . .

Astarte was a Syrian goddess but the ship is Greek and was built in Spain in 1973, trading as JUAN DE CARDONA until 1979. She is seen (right) approaching Swansea on 1 May 1987. Later that year, she was renamed PUCCINI under the Panamanian flag. Some scholars associate Astarte with the Greek goddess Aphrodite, who was known to the Romans as Venus. So, we look at UNION VENUS (below), built at Ringkobing in 1981, as she leaves Cardiff on 4 June 1986.

. . . AND GODS

UNION PLUTO is a sistership of UNION VENUS. She is seen (top) outward bound in the New Waterway on 31 May 1985, and, with mainmast lowered, she seems to have sailed from an upriver location. Pluto was the Roman god of the underworld and was one of three brothers. The other two were Neptune, god of the sea, and Jupiter, god of the upper world and generally considered to be the chief god. Our vessel is JUPITER (below) and she was built at Rendsburg in 1955. Renamed JUPITER B in 1983, her history since 1985 is sketchy. She was photographed in Goole's South Dock on 22 July 1980.

GREEK SHIPPING

Our previous theme of deities leads us easily to this photograph of OLYMPIOS APOLLON, our first view of shipping in Greece. The ship has an interesting history, having been built at Aarhus in 1961 as KATHOLM for DFDS, and sold to Finnish owners in 1968, being renamed KASTE. Her move to the Mediterranean and renaming took place in 1980, and I am unsure of her fate since 1982.

These two photographs were taken at the Peloponnese port of Nauplia on 17 August 1982. The Cypriot SERIFOS is seen loading the area's main export, namely fruit. She is another vessel whose earlier history can be easily traced but whose later life is more shadowy. She was built at Rendsburg in 1951 as HEIMO RECKMANN, changing her name to LOTHAR in 1965 and MILOS I in 1976. She took the name SERIFOS two years later.

The previous two photographs show that the Mediterranean is a rich source of interest for all ship enthusiasts, and it is one of the places where vessels of all kinds continue to find employment after being deemed surplus to requirements by owners elsewhere. Sadly, much traffic once handled by coasters has been transferred to ro/ro vessels, but there is nevertheless a considerable volume of bulk cargo handled by conventional coasters. Although the author has never experienced any problems, anyone proposing to visit Greece for ship photography should be warned that the Greeks can be inordinately sensitive. It is unfortunate that the Greek authorities find it difficult to understand that anyone can be interested in shipping.

The anchorages of Piraeus Roads are always occupied by vessels of all shapes and sizes. On 21 August 1982, I noted the interesting BOJNICE (above) built at Budapest in 1966 for the Czechoslovak Danube Shipping Company. Her low superstructure is clearly designed to permit navigation beneath low bridges.
Of very different profile is LILYMARE (below), seen on 8 August 1984 She was built at Gijon as BENIMAR in 1968, becoming MARIA ZAKELINA S in 1977 and LILYMARE in 1983.

The Panamanian-flagged CAP MALEAS is a liquefied gas tanker, although she began life as a dry cargo coaster, built at El Ferrol in 1958 as MAYPA. She remained under the Spanish flag until 1974, bearing the names CIBELES and ISLA DE MOURO. The turning point in her career came in 1965 when she was converted by the installation of six tanks to carry petroleum gas or anhydrous ammonia. The photograph (above) was taken on 8 August 1984.

On the previous day, I photographed the small tanker ALKION passing Perama, near Piraeus. In the heat of a Mediterranean summer, her icebreaker bow looks curiously out-of-place but it provides a good clue that she was built for trading in colder climes. In fact, she was built in 1950 at the Wartsila yard, Turku, and traded as ESSO FINLANDIA until 1971. Following a brief period called ISLA FINLANDIA, she found a permanent home in Greece in 1972.

Moored to the northern breakwater at the entrance to Piraeus harbour can usually be found several coasters awaiting cargoes. Often former British, Dutch or West German vesssels, these two views illustrate the potential interest - and the fact that not all the ships can be found in the reference books. On 21 August 1982, seven ships were on view, reading from left to right SEVASTIANNA H, AGIA ZONI, ILIOS 1, KALOVASI (or KALOVAS 1), GIANNIS, ZAKINTHOS (originally the Dutch NIAGARA), and half-visible at the extreme right ALMY, originally Everard's SONORITY.

There were only three ships to be seen on 7 August 1984. Again from left to right, we find TANE (originally the Dutch ANTILLA which became the British JOAN C), ANNA P (originally the West German VATERLAND) and PANAGIA FANEROMENI (again, West German in origin, having been the Sietas-built FLETH).

ISLE OF MAN

We stay with a geographical theme but move much nearer "home." It is often forgotten that the islands around our coast are visited by cargo ships as well as passenger ferries which are probably more familiar to the casual observer. We focus here on the Isle of Man and begin with two views of ships at the island's capital, Douglas. We see TRENTON moored at what is known as the Steam Packet Berth on 25 July 1988. She was built at Goole in 1964 as TRENTONIA for the Trent-based J. Wharton Ltd. (see p. 3). Her renaming in 1984 took little effort!

Tucked in at the eastern end of Victoria Pier and with a linkspan in the background is the Manx-owned MEDINA D on 10 April 1988. She dates from 1965 when built at Lowestoft as PLOVER for the General Steam Navigation Co. In 1971, she had her first Manx connection when she joined the fleet of the Ramsey Steamship Co. as BEN VEEN. She became MEDINA D in 1984. On 19 October 1988, she was abandoned by her crew in severe weather during a voyage from Rouen to Great Yarmouth and subsequently sank.

MEDINA D's port of registry was Ramsey and it is to that port that we now turn. Firstly, we find Glenlight Shipping's POLARLIGHT (above) inward bound on 3 September 1988. She dates from 1970 when she was built as WIGGS by J. R. Hepworth at Paull, on the Humber. After joining the Glenlight fleet, she was renamed and fitted with a deck crane in 1976. She sank, without loss of life, on 28 February 1989 when on passage to Ramsey with a cargo of cement.

Two regular island visitors are seen together here on 27 June 1988. The vessel in the background is TORA. Her hull is light grey undercoat because she had just been acquired by new owners, Mezeron Ltd., and would shortly be renamed GREEBA RIVER. She began life in 1969 as the Dutch APOLLO 1, becoming ARKLOW RIVER in 1980, CYNTHIA JUNE in 1982 and TORA in 1986. In the foreground is SILVER RIVER. Also owned by Mezeron, she dates from 1968 when built at Oldersum as SEACON. She became SEA TRENT in 1971, NATHURN in 1982 and SILVER RIVER in 1986. Both ships trade regularly between the island and mainland ports such as Glasson Dock, Anderton and Runcorn.

On the west coast of the island is Peel. It is the home of a small fishing fleet and is visited by coastal tankers and cargo vessels. In the latter category, Glenlight ships are the most frequent callers and we see (above) SEALIGHT using her "loglift" crane to good effect in the discharge of pipes. The photograph is dated 28 June 1988. SEALIGHT is a sistership of POLARLIGHT but was built as WIS by Malta Drydocks in 1970, joining Glenlight in 1975.

The call by Bowker and King's tanker BLACKROCK on 31 May 1989 was significant in that not only was the vessel herself new, having been launched at Selby on 8 February, but also she brought the first cargo for Total Oil's Isle of Man depot.

Waiting to load a cargo of scrap at Port St. Mary on 24 March 1989 is the Irish TARA SKY. In the absence of permanent cargo handling equipment, mobile cranes would have to be brought in. The vessel was built as MULCAIR at Hoogezand in 1958, and was renamed AARHUS in 1976, taking her current name in 1979.

All photographs in this section were taken by Albert Lowe.

The Honduran EOS was photographed at Castletown on 29 June 1988. She was built at Hamburg as EROS in 1957 and the R was deleted from her name in 1985. In the late 1960s, this south Manx port boasted a container service to Glasson Dock, but the port is now used infrequently by commercial shipping.

WHO IS HE?

Our next theme takes us back to ships' names. Vessels are often given names which relate to people. Those providing a surname offer no problem in identifying the lucky person to have a ship named after him/her. Those having simply a Christian name give no help. The person may be the owner or skipper's wife, or other family member. It could even be a pet rather than a person!

RUDYARD was built in Holland in 1960 as BLACKTHORN for Coe Shipping. In 1976, she was sold to Effluent Services Ltd. and converted to, as Lloyd's Register says, a "mud carrier." Seen at Birkenhead on 28 August 1979, she became JANE SEA in 1980.

HENDRIK (below) was photographed heading up the Elbe on 30 May 1984. Built at Leer in 1965 and lengthened in 1974, she is certainly worth including in a section on names because she was called DORIS between 1970 and 1978, having begun life as GEBINA.

OLIVIER (above) is a real multinational. Built in Holland in 1986, she (?he) flies the Dutch flag, is owned by the Swedish company of Erik Thun and bears the French words "Vieille Montagne" (Old Mountains) on her bridge. She is seen arriving in Cardiff to load coke on 15 August 1988.

The small pilot boat at the Dee port of Mostyn does its best to push the Austrian STEFAN towards the quayside on 1 June 1988. She was built at Setoda in Japan as SANDERSKOPPEL for West German owners in 1977, her change of flag and ownership coming in 1986.

WHO IS SHE?

Moving to the ladies now, and our first sighting is at Goole. Entering Ocean Lock on a cold January day in 1980 is EDNA. A typical Sietas-built ship, she dates from 1958 when she was launched as THYRA BEHRENS, her name change coming in 1979. Unusually, she was bought by owners in Paraguay in 1982 and was renamed AREGUA. Despite this, she spent 1983 trading between the U.K. and near-Continent, and probably never ventured anywhere near her new "home" country. She left Queenborough on 14 March 1984 for the Danish port of Graasten where she was eventually scrapped.

KATHE-MARIE, passing Cuxhaven on 27 May 1979, was built at Hamburg in 1952 and lengthened in 1956. In 1981, she hoisted the flag of Ghana when renamed BONSO, this being changed to CAMCO STAR in 1985.

A rather different kind of ship, but yet another from, yes, the Sietas yard. This vessel (above) was built in 1971 and was photographed heading up the Ship Canal towards Manchester when on charter to Manchester Liners for their Mediterranean service. Taking the name MARGRET in 1976, she had previously been HANNES KNUPPEL, PINTO and MARGRET KNUPPEL. Since 1984 she has been owned in Finland and has had the name SKANDEN.

The connections of BETTY-JEAN are all British. She dates from 1985 and is an example of a highly-successful coaster design from the Yorkshire Drydock Co. in Hull, a city which is also the base of her owners, John Whitaker Ltd. The photograph shows her at Perth on 29 July 1987.

BRIDGES

A combination of careful planning, good fortune and considerable patience are often needed to photograph ships passing through or beneath bridges. We begin at Kingsferry Bridge which joins the Isle of Sheppey to the mainland. It was opened in 1959 and carries road and rail traffic. Passing along the Swale from Ridham Dock towards the Medway on 6 August 1989 is VANERNSEE, built at Leer in 1983.

With so few ships now trading to Norwich or Cantley, opportunities to see ships passing the railway bridge over the Yare at Reedham are very limited. It was on 30 July 1983 that I captured on film the West German GORCH FOCK outward bound in ballast from Norwich. Built by Sietas in 1966, she has traded as ESPERANZA B since 1984.

We move up the east coast to the Ouse to find the Polish NER passing Boothferry road bridge on her way to Selby on 7 August 1983. Subsequently sold to Honduran-flag interests, she unusually retained her name and eventually in November 1984 arrived at Pasajes where demolition began in January 1986.

There are three bridges to mention in this photograph taken on the Manchester Ship Canal. In the top left hand corner is Latchford railway viaduct and immediately beneath it is Knutsford Road swing bridge just opening to allow the passage of SHELL DIRECTOR on 28 July 1980. The third bridge is that on which I was standing - Latchford High Level Bridge. The ship was built at Appledore in 1972. She bore the name CAERNARVON until 1979.

The two photographs on this page depict the Gloucester Ship Canal whose fairly narrow bridges have given many a captain an anxious moment. Passing the Pilot Inn at Quedgeley on the outskirts of Gloucester on 2 May 1983 is THRUSCROSS, a Dutch-built tanker dating from 1954. She had had the name STELLA MARIS from her launch until 1971, and thence CONSTANCE until 1977. Her end came when she was demolished at Milford Haven in late 1988.

We have already seen HOOP on page 27. In this view, we find her during the same voyage as she approaches Purton Lower Bridge, having just negotiated a tight turn in the Canal.

It is not always realised that a considerable amount of shipping uses the River Itchen in Southampton. Passing beneath the bridge which connects Woolston to the city is the sand dredger GLEN GOWER, built at Foxhol in 1963. She has kept her name for 27 years, although she operated out of Swansea until the early 1980s. The photograph was taken on 29 May 1990.

We stay with sand dredgers as we look at probably the most famous bridge in this section. Brunel's Clifton Suspension Bridge over the River Avon in Bristol was completed in 1864. The only commercial vessels to pass beneath it, apart from the passenger ships WAVERLEY and BALMORAL, are sand dredgers. HARRY BROWN survives in mid-1990 as one of the oldest of this breed still working the rich dredging grounds of the Bristol Channel. She was built locally at Charles Hill's yard in 1962.

BENEATH THAMES BRIDGES

Although the last three decades have seen a massive decrease in the number of seagoing vessels in the Thames upstream of the Pool of London, there have been recent signs that the trend is being reversed to some extent, although there will never be a return to former volumes of trade simply because many of the riverside wharves and associated warehouses have been "redeveloped". Ironically, the many commercial and residential developments undertaken in the late 1980s have ensured a steady demand for sand and aggregates, and it is still possible to see small vessels conveying these commodities navigating beneath the Thames bridges, particularly on weekday flood tides. Dredgers and large tank barges are also to be found. Hall Dredging Ltd. has long been associated with the sand trade from Essex, and JOSEPH HALL is seen (right) heading upstream with a full cargo. She was built at J. W. Cook's Wivenhoe yard in 1963.

Departing in ballast is ROFFEN, built on the Medway in 1965 and originally owned by Crescent Shipping.

Built in 1969 for Crescent Shipping at its own yard at Strood is LIBATION (above).

Slightly smaller than LIBATION is CAPTION, built for Crescent Shipping by Richard Dunston at Hessle in 1963. Both ships have now left the ownership of Crescent Shipping although they retain their original names. All four photographs in this section were taken during a half hour spell on 10 August 1989.

RUSSIAN SHIPS

The Russian merchant fleet is vast and it difficult to select a few examples of the coasters which operate within it. The oldest of the four ships chosen is GAUYA. She dates from 1959 and was one of the last examples to be built of a design which was first introduced in 1937. She was built at Budapest. This photograph was taken as she approached Exmouth on 19 April 1984.

One of a class of twenty ships, SOVIETSKIY POGRANICHNIK is seen heading towards Cardiff on 24 April 1986. She was built at Nikolayev in 1970.

FRITSIS ROZIN was built at Boizenburg in East Germany in 1971. A handy, multi-purpose ship, she can handle containers as well as bulk cargoes. This photograph shows her in the River Mersey on 15 September 1979.

Included in the Russian fleet are several classes of ships designed for navigation on inland seas and waterways. The "Ladoga" class, for instance, was initially designed with a capability of sailing south from Leningrad to the Caspian Sea and Iran. Ladoga itself is a large inland lake north-east of Leningrad. On 27 May 1987, LADOGA 17 was photographed passing Rozenburg on the New Waterway. She was built in Finland in 1979, and differs from the first vessels in the class in having a higher superstructure.

TANKER TRAFFIC

Until 1979, Shell and BP had a joint marketing agreement and shared a fleet of coastal tankers which were named after refineries or coastal distribution depots. In that year, however, the two companies each went their separate ways and vessels were renamed as necessary. TEESPORT (below), a 1966 product of the Grangemouth Dockyard Co., became SHELL TRADER. She is seen at Eastham in August 1970, heading for Stanlow to load another cargo of refined products.

At the same location on 26 July 1989 is SHELL SEAFARER, built at Goole in 1981.

Once again, the two photographs on this page are at the same location, but only a matter of minutes apart despite the different weather conditions. In the upper picture, BP HARRIER is about to pass beneath the Forth road bridge as she heads for Grangemouth. She was built at Appledore in 1980. Completing the quartet of oil company-owned vessels is ESSO AVON, built at Groningen in 1981.

The previous two photographs were taken on 12 April 1983. On the same occasion, we now look towards the attractive village of North Queensferry as we view Rowbotham's ORIONMAN outward bound from Grangemouth. She was built at Aberdeen in 1975.

The name of Bowker and King has long been associated with estuarial tankers and tank barges. During the 1980s the firm expanded and has built up a handy fleet of coastal tankers including new ships as well as second-hand tonnage. Exemplifying the fleet, however, is the bunkering tanker BARRIER, built by J. Pollock at Faversham in 1958 and attracting the attention of onlookers as she approaches the harbour entrance at Portsmouth on 26 July 1988. She underwent reconstruction in 1982, for she was built with bridge amidships. Bowker and King is now part of the Hays Group and the fleet has been merged with that of Crescent Shipping under the latter's nominal ownership.

J. H. Whitaker Ltd., is another firm to be expanding from estuarial craft to larger vessels. Built at Wroclaw as LUBAN for Polish owners in 1976, WHITANK joined the Whitaker fleet in 1987 and is seen on 7 August 1989 at Ramsgate where she is a regular caller.

PASS OF GLENOGLE (left) was built at Sunderland in 1963 and worked as a tanker for the first twelve years of her life. She was converted to a sand dredger in 1975 and is to be seen in Bristol Channel ports as SAND SAPPHIRE. She was photographed in her original guise on 10 September 1972 at Partington Basin on the Manchester Ship Canal.

TWO FOR THE PRICE OF ONE

For several reasons, photographs depicting more than one vessel have an appeal all of their own. They enable comparisons to be made in terms of design, size and age, and they can make for interesting photographs in themselves. Kendall's Wharf in Langstone Harbour on 26 July 1988 is the setting for this view of two interesting sand dredgers To the right is Kendall's own KBII, which was built in 1960 at Foxhol as GLEN HAFOD for Bristol Channel owners. She was bought by Kendall Brothers in 1985 and renamed. On the left is HEXHAMSHIRE LASS whose life began in 1955 at Charles Hill's Bristol yard. As her name suggests, she originally worked in the north-east of England and was usually to be found on the River Tyne. She was converted for sand dredging in 1973.

We move to the River Neath as MARTINDYKE, heading out to the Bristol Channel, passes the gas tanker MELROSE which has just arrived to load at BP's Baglan Bay jetty on 22 September 1984. MARTINDYKE, built at Goole in 1975, became RUTLAND in 1988. MELROSE has retained her original name since her construction at Oldenburg in 1971.

On 19 February 1988, TORA passes the Faroese ATLANTIC CLOUD at the entrance to Glasson Dock. The latter vessel was built at Skala in 1965 as ARNATINDUR, her name change coming in 1986. We have already seen TORA on page 55.

Hurrying beneath the Humber Bridge on 4 May 1986 are SEA TAMAR, built at Papenburg in 1984, and ANGELIQUE V, built three years earlier at Foxhol.

SHIPS IN THE LANDSCAPE

Ship enthusiasts tend to be a conservative lot and still consider the three-quarter bow photograph of a ship, without any background, to be the ideal. While admitting that a forest of dockside cranes can make for a cluttered background, it must not be forgotten that dockside views can be of great importance in terms of history, geography, architecture and industrial archaeology. Furthermore, while we consider the open sea to be the natural habitat of ships, this is certainly not always the case and a ship passing through the landscape can convey a sense of drama which at times verges on the surreal. Such is not claimed for the following selection of photographs, but it is hoped that it may encourage ship enthusiasts - and photographers - to search for alternative viewpoints.

The declaration that the port of Scarborough would close to commercial trade in 1989 proved, thankfully, to be premature. Coasters have continued to call, albeit much less frequently. The attractive houses of the harbour town contrast with the typical seafront shops, cafes and amusement arcades while the 12th century castle looks down impassively on the scene. In this photograph (right), dated 16 May 1981, the West German GABRIELLA, built at Wewelsfleth in 1973, has just arrived with a cargo of timber while TWEBRO passes through the harbour entrance. Built at Appingedam in 1964, her appearance has been spoiled by the removal of her mainmast. She currently flies the Honduran flag as RESIDU.

We travel about 30 km. north from Scarborough to the port of Whitby which is, in fact, owned by Scarborough Borough Council. On 7 August 1985 the West German ESTE leaves the harbour bound for Ipswich. High on the East Cliff in the background are the ruins of Whitby Abbey and, to the right, St. Mary's Parish Church. The vessel was built at Emden in 1966 as REALTA. She became CLAUS JURGEN in 1975 and ESTE in 1980.

TOR BAY (above), having navigated through Torbay, passes the Ness at Shaldon on 28 September 1986 as she negotiates the tricky entrance to Teignmouth where she will load a cargo of ball clay for the Middle East. She was built at Foxhol in 1967 and sailed as BRUNDLUND until 1979.

Hurrying past the smart residences on the banks of the Elbe is the Swedish tanker TARINA II, a venerable veteran dating from 1929 and still going strong when this photograph was taken on 29 May 1986.

(Above) On 14 October 1989, ATLANTIC CLOUD makes a splendid sight as she dashes westwards through the Sound of Mull. We have just seen this coaster on page 75.

The barren hills of Ardgour on the western bank of Loch Linnhe form the backdrop for the Irish MURELL as she makes her way towards Corpach to discharge pulp at the paper mill on 4 August 1987. Built at Brattvag in 1973, she has traded as HOXA SOUND for Dennison Shipping since mid-1988.

SAINT ORAN, owned by J. and A. Gardner, is a true multi-purpose vessel, having side tanks and ro/ro capacity in addition to her conventional hold for bulk cargoes. On 7 April 1986, she loaded roadstone for Tiree at Gardner's own quarry at Bonawe on the northern shore of Loch Etive. This photograph (above) shows her leaving the loch and about to pass beneath the Connel Ferry Bridge.

Several photographs in this book were taken at Eastham where the Manchester Ship Canal meets the River Mersey. A country park and panoramic views make this a popular location with the general public as well as ship enthusiasts. The photographers tend to stay by the water's edge and miss out on the opportunities offered by stepping back a few metres. The tanker ECHOMAN, built at Appledore in 1982 and owned by Rowbotham Tankships Ltd., approaches the Ship Canal entrance on 12 August, 1983.

Index of Ships' Names

Postscript

This book has been produced in response to the many requests which I have received since the publication of "Coasters around Britain". Sadly, it has not proved possible to include photographs of ships in Irish ports, the Channel Islands or the Isle of Wight. Should the opportunity arise to produce a further pictorial book about coasters (and I sincerely hope that it will), every effort will be made to fill some of these gaps.

I must thank the many individuals who have helped make this book possible, in particular Ian Willett and Albert Lowe for their contributions. I would like to give special thanks also to Richard Potter who has checked many of my facts, but I claim personal and sole credit for all the mistakes. Compiling a book such as this could not be done without help offered by the magazines "Sea Breezes" and "Ships Monthly", the World Ship Society and its journal "Marine News", Yorkshire Ship Enthusiasts and its quarterly newsletter, and Lloyd's Register of Shipping. The team at Beacon Printers once again deserves thanks and praise for all the effort put into design and production. To my family, I offer sympathy in having a ship enthusiast as a son/husband/father but I thank them for their patience, understanding and support.

BERNARD McCALL